THE SEA, ONCE IT
CASTS ITS SPELL,
HOLDS ONE IN ITS
NET OF WONDER
FOREVER.

- Jacques-Yves Cousteau -

The ocean, the beach, the sand and the sea... It is here, in this wild and wonderful place, that we find the true beauty of life. It is here, with friends and family nearby, that every moment becomes a memory.

With this guest book, you're invited to take some time, relax, and write down whatever feels meaningful to you—perhaps a favorite memory or something you discovered during your stay. Whatever you choose, the words you write will create a record and a celebration of your time here—words that will be treasured for years to come.

Welcome, and enjoy.

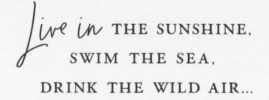

Live in THE SUNSHINE,
SWIM THE SEA,
DRINK THE WILD AIR...

- Ralph Waldo Emerson -

On the beach,

YOU CAN LIVE IN BLISS.

- Dennis Wilson -

THE TIME TO BE
HAPPY IS NOW,
THE PLACE TO BE
HAPPY IS HERE...

- Robert G. Ingersoll -

How beautiful it is

TO DO NOTHING, AND THEN

TO REST AFTERWARD.

- Spanish Proverb -

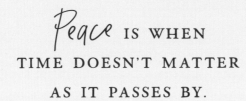

Peace IS WHEN
TIME DOESN'T MATTER
AS IT PASSES BY.

- Maria Schell -

AT THE BEACH, LIFE IS DIFFERENT.
TIME DOESN'T MOVE HOUR TO HOUR BUT MOOD
TO MOMENT. WE LIVE BY THE CURRENTS,
plan by the tides and follow the sun.

- Unknown -

KEEP YOUR

FACE TO THE

SUNSHINE...

- Paul B. Armstrong -

Smile,

BREATHE AND GO SLOWLY.

- Thich Nhat Hanh -

...*There is* NO GREATER JOY THAN TO HAVE AN ENDLESSLY CHANGING HORIZON, FOR EACH DAY TO HAVE A NEW AND DIFFERENT SUN.

- Christopher McCandless -

Be happy in the moment,

THAT'S ENOUGH. EACH MOMENT
IS ALL WE NEED, NOT MORE.

- Mother Teresa -

...I'VE GOT
NOTHING TO
DO TODAY
BUT SMILE.

- Paul Simon -

FIND WHAT BRINGS YOU JOY

and go there.

- Jan Phillips -

THE WAVES OF THE SEA
HELP ME GET BACK TO ME.

- Jill Davis -

Stop every now and then.

JUST STOP AND ENJOY.

TAKE A DEEP BREATH.

RELAX AND TAKE IN THE

ABUNDANCE OF LIFE.

- Anonymous -

Breathe
AND LET BE...

- Jon Kabat-Zinn -

The less routine the more life.

- Amos Bronson Alcott -

WE ARE TIED TO THE OCEAN.
AND WHEN WE GO BACK TO THE
SEA—WHETHER IT IS TO SAIL OR
TO WATCH IT—WE ARE GOING
BACK FROM WHENCE WE CAME.

- John F. Kennedy -

ALWAYS LEAVE ENOUGH
ROOM IN YOUR LIFE
TO DO SOMETHING THAT
makes you happy...

- Paul Hawken -

Let the beauty

OF WHAT YOU LOVE

BE WHAT YOU DO.

- Rumi -

I go to the ocean

TO CALM DOWN, TO RECONNECT...

TO JUST BE HAPPY.

- Nnedi Okorafor -

DON'T HURRY,
DON'T WORRY.

- Walter Hagen -

Life's too short

TO BE SPENT HAVING ANYTHING BUT FUN.

- Sylvia Dee -

IF YOU WANT TO BE HAPPY,

BE SO.

- Kozma Prutkov -

Be content with what you have;

REJOICE IN THE WAY THINGS ARE.

- Lao Tzu -

The ocean STIRS THE HEART, INSPIRES THE IMAGINATION AND BRINGS ETERNAL JOY TO THE SOUL.

- Wyland -

...be intent

UPON THE PERFECTION

OF THE PRESENT DAY...

- William Law -

LOVE THE MOMENT AND THE
ENERGY OF THAT MOMENT WILL
SPREAD BEYOND ALL BOUNDARIES
INTO BLISSFUL, *peaceful happiness.*

- Corita Kent -

Having fun

IS SIMPLY HOLDING ON TO
THE JOY OF EACH DAY.

– Judith Harlan –

THERE WAS A MAGIC ABOUT THE SEA.
PEOPLE WERE DRAWN TO IT. PEOPLE
WANTED TO LOVE BY IT, SWIM IN IT,
PLAY IN IT, LOOK AT IT.

- Cecelia Ahern -

Follow your bliss.

– Joseph Campbell –

Live in THE PRESENT MOMENT
AND FIND YOUR INTEREST AND
HAPPINESS IN THE THINGS OF TODAY.

- Emmet Fox -

...THERE ARE TIMES WHEN WE STOP.
WE SIT STILL... WE LISTEN AND BREEZES
FROM A WHOLE OTHER WORLD
begin to whisper.

- James Carroll -

SOMETIMES THE MOST
IMPORTANT THING IN
A WHOLE DAY IS THE
REST WE TAKE BETWEEN
TWO DEEP BREATHS...

- Etty Hillesum -

In this moment,

THERE IS PLENTY OF TIME. IN THIS MOMENT,
YOU ARE PRECISELY AS YOU SHOULD BE.
IN THIS MOMENT, THERE IS INFINITE POTENTIAL.

- Victoria Moran -

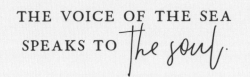

THE VOICE OF THE SEA
SPEAKS TO *the soul*.

- Kate Chopin -

Our memories of the ocean
WILL LINGER ON, LONG AFTER OUR
FOOTPRINTS IN THE SAND ARE GONE.

- Anonymous -

COMPENDIUM.
live inspired

WRITTEN BY: AMELIA RIEDLER
DESIGNED BY: SARAH FORSTER
EDITED BY: KRISTIN EADE

ISBN: 978-1-946873-05-7

2nd printing. Printed in China with soy inks.

Create meaningful moments with gifts that inspire.

CONNECT WITH US
live-inspired.com | sayhello@compendiuminc.com

@compendiumliveinspired
#compendiumliveinspired